# Living the Outskirts

*poems by*

# Susan E. Hamilton

*Finishing Line Press*
Georgetown, Kentucky

# Living the Outskirts

## ACKNOWLEDGMENTS

*Power Lines*, Informed Consent, Finishing Line Press, 2018

*Abandoned Homestead, Untitled (Figure in Landscape) West Wind Review:*
*Conditions* (1993), Southern Oregon State College, Ashland, OR

Thank you to my teachers, especially those at the U of WA and Hugo House, Seattle.

Publisher: Leah Huete de Maines
Editor: Christen Kincaid
Cover Photo: Susan E. Hamilton
Author Photo: Parents of Susan E. Hamilton
Cover Design: Elizabeth Maines McCleavy


Order online: www.finishinglinepress.com
also available on amazon.com

Author inquiries and mail orders:
Finishing Line Press
PO Box 1626
Georgetown, Kentucky 40324
USA

# Contents

*To Small Towns Everywhere*

## Painted near the Purdy Cutoff

The cows in the valley must have been hard
to render, they are so small, and yet it's obvious
they're cows. I pause at the barn daily, the scene
in oil over my mantel in Seattle of the Olympic
Mountains, drowning here in urban effluent.

I'm no martyr. No bumper
stickers on my car or buttons on my hat.
The apathetic are heretics, I know that.
My skin drips off me like Crisco every
morning as I read the paper. I've given up.
I've let invasive ivy fill my head with knots.

I remember climbing the snow chute
on Mt. Ellinor, and how The Brothers looked
like a single cusp from Shelton, yet like twins
when seen from Seattle. In my living room
I stand at the silo beside that barn on the Skokomish,
wish for the outskirts of a small town,
for garter snakes coiled on the compost heap,
for Mom calling us home with the 3-short
1-long blast of her whistle.

## Broken Snakes

Bowl-cut bangs and chipped incisors, Ruzo
held one end of the rope. Her sister Rhoda, a Ruzo
with glasses and giggles, toyed with the other.
The rope straddled the road next to the entrance
of our camp. Danny watched from there,
where we had abandoned buried mason
jars full of filbert husks (money) and
pits covered with fir boughs (traps). Not
long ago Danny and I had pulled down our pants, confirming
whispers, but who cared. The mirage of hot asphalt
bristled with sticks thrust in the melted tar
of plugged potholes. Garter carcasses
desiccated in esses nearby. Danny did that.
Unless I was there to protest.

The rope serpentined lazily. Who could cross the false
finish line before it flashed between her legs? I tripped,
falling sideways on the gravel shoulder. My right wing
snapped, a door now stuck ajar. Mom helped my limp arm
into a clean blouse for the doctor.

I wore the harness for weeks, reining in
that clavicle. The camp stagnated, tar untouched,
Danny scowling. Snakes were sacrificed.
And when I was cut free, the harness straps
had sliced both armpits, balls of muscles
extruding like pink snails.
My father screamed at the doctor.
I was frightened. I'd thought healing was meant
to hurt. I thought of the snakes
cooling on asphalt.

## My Last Picture Show

I insisted on wearing my church gloves
last night to the Babe Blue Ox Theater,
it being the last picture show I'd see there.

Paul Bunyan had dropped into Shelton
about a hundred years prior. A few swings of his ax
cleared the valley from upper Goldsborough Creek
to Hammersley Inlet and then Paul put
Babe to work dragging fallen giants on a skid
road to Oakland Bay. Babe did such a good job
that Paul built the folks of Shelton a movie theater
and named it for Babe. It wasn't long before she
was replaced with the logging train. Sometimes
I walk the trestle on the way to school. I don't break
stride, the blur of rapids only twenty feet
below the ties. Mom would ground me if she knew.
The train snakes to Camp Grisdale, brings
back skinny trees with the big ones now.
The rusted skeleton of the pulp mill was razed.
Daddy said the digesters were five stories high.

And now I've gone and lost my glove at Babe's
Blue Ox Theater while watching *Thomasina*. I think
the veterinarian in that movie just didn't like animals,
but that witch in the glen sure did.
I hope Babe headed to her place.


*Thomasina*, a movie in which a "witch" saves a cat after a veterinarian's
failure.

3

## Hammersley Inlet

In the 50's the pulp mill shut,
oysters the size of quarters
assumed to be drowning in effluent.
The research lab lasted longer
giving Dad a job advising mills
endangered, not yet extinct.

Last smokestack felled in the 60's,
the lumber mill no longer incinerating
second growth tailings. Gone
the fly ash of childhood, pepper flakes
on Mom's white sheets stiff with July,
surrendering on the line.

Summer in the 70's, sticky nights
throbbing with the whine of band saws
riding updrafts over Angleside.
Whistles marking day, swing, graveyard—
friends in hard hats, caulk boots,
pulling lumber off the green chain,
wet wood the heaviest.

## The Weeping Fir, Shelton Valley

Near the woods where we nudged
chanterelles from their moss bunting
stood The Weeping Fir. A crude sign
labeled the obvious amid its happy cohort
along the road. By all traits a Douglas fir, yet
its branch tips drooped earthward as if grieving
the fate awaiting all trees, clear-cuts edging closer.
What of the house built of The Weeping Fir?
Did siding blister, the roof sag,
did studs cry amber tears?
Were the children sad like me,
on the drive home?

## Midden, Mason County

I
Sunday afternoons we paid the toll,
that's all it took to gain entrance as county residents.
The guy in the booth, his dark dog drooling in the grass nearby, swung
the gate upward and our station wagon descended
one-lane one-way into the chaos and stench of the pit.

Think the word *pyre*.
The bulldozed hummocks smoldered with tubeless skulls of TVs,
torsos of washers and dryers, severed fluorescent bulbs. Flames
were sporadic. What to burn and what to bury? Who decided
where and when? I knew the why. We offered contents of two battered
aluminum drums: milk cartons, kitchen peels, stems, seeds, eggshells, carcasses,
scales, bones, marrow, rock, paper, scissors. I brought pages from my diary
to stoke embers but scattered my days instead at gulls circling the fumaroles.
No, it's wasn't Wonder Bread and they brayed like harpies
at the uselessness of written words.

I was chubby, I had bangs, and wore corrective shoes.
Marley Henly always said *hi* to my shoes when we passed
in the hall. They were oxfords with the insoles built-up to tip
me in the right direction. I was tired of the right direction. I poked
around the dump for Mary Janes but knew the likelihood of finding left
and right was slim. Maybe I could find a teddy bear to clean up and give my
older sister so the one we shared could be all mine. I'd named him Tim,
and he was my best friend.

## II

I miss the dump. Resent the tidy transfer station that separates
me from hell on earth. Without mud to fossilize dregs,
I've begun to burn photos, force memory to carry its load.
In wraiths of dream-remembering, I find Mrs. Rollins,
my babysitter (long dead), perched on a doorless fridge.
She is surrounded by milk glass we gave her on special occasions
and offers me a pink wintergreen mint from the candy dish
she kept on a crocheted doily. She tells me that my husband's grandmother
Gladie wasn't always so dour.
*It was more than hard for Gladie to lose her husband before*
*her only child was born. Go gentler in thought and quit*
*drinking bad wine every time you think of Gladie.*
As penance, I comb a pile of glass splinters and find an old elixir vial,
once part of Gladie's bottle collection. When I awake,
I will unleash its contents—tell my husband
Shelton wasn't such a bad place to grow up.

## Shelton Postcard, ©1960

He's a jovial 2-D Santa
with a bag of Mason County
products: Simpson lumber
Rayonier research, a Christmas Tree,
and a dolly whose face
can become yours.
Welcome to Shelton,
Christmastown, USA.
The freeze sets needles
perfectly here; three million
trees harvested each season.
On a sunny day we'd cut
our own up Northcliff, the forest
exuding smells of wholesomeness.
Hibernation was good for this
small-town girl. Nostalgia
bleeds like a postmark,
pentimento underfoot.

## Living the Outskirts

I want the pulpy thickened pea-soup taste
of a green between bright and sage. To strain
the ham chunks through teeth and chew
sandwiches of dandelion leaves gathered
that morning, their yellow counterparts
glowing in the silver sugar bowl
turned vase.

I want to smell the ozone, hear her *Singer*
whir the smocking, dresses worn in sandbox
and on swings. To see her in her embroidered
dirndl next to velvet holly hocks
against the deepness of firs across the dead
end road, our woods nonstop
to the Pacific.

I want to watch him shave, each swath
plowing snow across his cheeks and chin
and neck. Scarlet center of a tissue piece, the nick,
or fingertips of wild strawberries beyond
the picket fence along the trail to the wooden
water tower he climbed the night
he rescued Inky.

*If luck is the crystal of design, who do we thank*
*for serendipity?* I want to dance inside the rings
of small white caps and stipes, Venn diagram
of our lives against the meadow
on the outskirts.

## Batstone Funeral Home

From bone china cups we drank tea Mom made as we sat near the husk of Dad,
waiting for the undertaker we'd known since Sunday School. Brad drove
the mile up Angleside to our house, spoke in a cadence of condolence,
ushered in the black bag on a gurney with straps to keep a body earth bound.
We backed down the hall into the kitchen as Brad and his assistant lifted
Dad, sheet and all, into the vinyl maw. We waited for the sound of zipping,
moved to the living room window to watch him head
out the front door on Grant Avenue for the last time.

We met Brad later at Batstone's, 7th and Railroad. The Batstone girls,
Dotty and Polly, had gone to Sunday School too. They had plaited pigtails
and looked like twins. We wondered what they thought of their uncle
running the only funeral parlor in town. Brad asked questions to rough
an obit and attend to physical trappings for entry into the hereafter. We chose
hymns, psalms, testament readings, old and new.
We spurned an urn; a paper bag would do.
Dad would be meandering the Pacific.

We walked the couple blocks along Railroad to Ming Tree's,
nodded to Mrs. Chen, picked up takeout like Dad would
for a special occasion. Bought the box of candied ginger
like he would, as a treat for Mom.

### Rogers School, 1950's

Beyond the gate from the old commander's
house where we rent on the northern
outskirts of town, wild strawberries
lead to the wooden water tower and
the playground at Rogers School.

Some imagine vacant
eyes at the windows of the clapboard
building watching us trespass
on Sunday afternoon. But we've been
to church and know better—
their eyes are eager,
not vacant.

We tug the metal
uprights on the hexagonal
merry-go-round, urging the sluggish
wooden wheel to spin. We run alongside
in the well-worn circle, jumping
aboard as the churlish
nausea takes holds,
then leaves us giddy.

No one mentions Rogers
School at my school.
Like the *Exceptional
Foresters* on the southern
outskirts of town no one
talks about either.
But on any weekday at Rogers,
we'd be right there with them all,
riding 'til we puked.


Rogers School, a school for Special Needs children

## The Bosco Sundae

The tiny sundae melted further
through tears she couldn't help.
She'd told him she wanted just a little one,
and Daddy thought it such a joke—

In front of her, he placed
a teaspoon of ice cream, lost
in a green Melmac soup bowl, lopsided
dollop of dark brown Bosco chocolate
drizzling off its pathetic peak.

Mom, Dad, sisters, jeered in disbelief—
her tears instead of laughter.

Making matters worse,
they'd tell her the rest of her life,
*You never could take a joke.*

## Perry Mason and Aunt Edie

We walked home slowly after the bomb drill, *what if'ing*
aloud, imagining the roiling cloud turning itself inside
out and raining our bodies as cinders along the trail.
I wondered, Aunt Edie, if you'd be crying again when I got home.

It had only been a year since that day in November
when radios got through on the playground and we gave up
4-square in stunned silence. JFK was bleeding to death in Dallas.
I came through the backdoor and you met me on the landing coming
up from the basement where you ironed Dad's shirts, our sheets, tablecloths,
dishtowels, and our homemade dresses while watching Perry Mason. Regular
programming had been interrupted and you were in tears. It was scary because
you didn't cry. And if you did, it gave you nose bleeds.

Aunt Edie, I think of Perry's earnestness and Della's kindness,
Paul's dapper sleuthing, Hamilton Burger's craggy face, of dampened laundry
rolled carefully in your plastic ironing basket, the steaming iron, the smell
like crisped toast as you pressed. I think of the edging on our white sheets
you patterned with the applique attachment on your Singer, the storeroom
filled with fabric scraps, excesses of toilet paper, paper towels, toothpaste,
your jars of preserves, the bearded leftovers
in the back of the fridge.

Aunt Edie, the cold war warmed for a while, but cold returns in cycles.
There may never be enough toilet paper or toothpaste, nor enough
food in the pantry. Permanent press will replace ironing, and preserves
will come in cans, but Perry will survive in the reruns,
winning his cases again and again.

## The Lord's Prayer Ends in Sour Pie Cherries

I picked sour pie cherries for Mom
with a thoroughness to absolve the worst in me
for at least a day.
I thrust the ladder to heights above earth
I could never reach by mere climbing.
My eyes were filled with the sun bouncing off the red-orange
roundness of those cherries in my stainless bowl.
The sour sting of their flesh filled my mouth.
I tried to behave myself with the pits.

Why all this should have made me wonder at ten
about *forever and ever*
I cannot to this day know.
I wandered into the kitchen and asked Mom,
*But how do we live forever?*
Without pausing as she cut the butter, cinnamon,
and brown sugar into tiny balls of cobbler topping,
she answered, without looking up,
*Now don't go worrying about things we can't begin to understand.*

I let the screen door slam back into the blazes of mid-afternoon.
Back to the cherries, hanging in doubles and brave singles.
No ladder now, I liked the rough bark of the branch assigned to me.

Sleep did not come easy after my epiphany.
The bathroom nightlight could not begin
to pierce the horror of *world without end, forever and ever.*
As if homework, vacuuming, and teeth brushing would never cease.
As if we could never just lay-me-down for good.

Next day, I picked at least two extra quarts of sour pie cherries
to give to our neighbors
as unto ourselves,
Amen.

### Dante Visits Shelton, circa 1960s

*I.      Rat Bonking at the Garbage Dump*

The frantic rats disperse as gulls cajole
and gangs arrive from town with pipes and bats
to bonk the rodents near the fumaroles

of burning garbage, rotting food, and all that
humans waste in want of something more,
then toss into the infinite crevasse.

That rodents cannot share the store
of sustenance these human hoods discard
is wrong, and so that order is restored

these goons will spend their nights perusing dregs,
sate their hunger sucking worm bin slop
and wish they'd drunk far fewer kegs.


*II.      Friday Night Football*

In helmets, pads, spiked cleats, and plastic maille
the burly blockers line up center front
and face-off on the unturfed field in rain.

These gladiators call the cues in grunts
while mud obscures identity, and teammates joust
with teammates, forcing one at last to punt...

The spectators, not knowing who to boo,
scream louder than before, *who won?*
but frankly, all they really want is blood-

letting and vertebrae compression. In unison
the crowd pays homage to the fray but leaves
unsated, no bodies in the end zone.

*III.*     *Graduation*

Blackened specks belch daily from the stack
ascended by the grads at night with ropes and hooks,
and cans of orange spray paint in their packs.

Three hundred feet above the valley floor,
*they* watch the town's one stoplight green to red
and scoff that Satan did not offer Jesus more

than lofty heights and damn nice views. Instead
they would have handed him a beer!
But for such insolence this gang will learn to dread

the very height above the floor their beds
are raised. Their garish "X" in paint against
the stack will be forgotten long before it fades.

## Lobshroom

She lurks beneath an apse
of hemlock, eager for first rains
to waken thirst for stipe and cap
she cannot grow herself.
She is *Hypomyces lactifluorum*.
No myth of mycology is she.
A fungal cannibal, she seeks
the sullen *Rusula*, the innocent
*Luctifluus*, smothers these less-than-
savory sisters with her veil
until she becomes
the lobster mushroom.
She thickens stipes, coats their alabaster
with cooked crustacean orange,
lures with faint smell of fish
the hunters who seek her flesh,
her contorted crimson underfoot.
She rejoices in her monstrosity,
their culinary godsend.
With time, she'll cloak
all mushrooms with her pall,
erupt between the toes
of hunting humans, turn
their feet to claws, imbue
them with piscean scent.

## Junior Lifesaving Class

I thought I'd left Donna behind, remembered instead
those *Paydays* for a dime before the bus ride home, but
there she sits in the dank cement changing room among
wire baskets, combination locks, and chlorine reek in all her
indifference that I now recognize as adolescent smugness.
She's real, no matter how she gets inside my head.
She grabs me from behind in the pool, an elbow chokehold—
our practice of the front-approach rescue now become
the dreaded rear head-hold. But that was Donna Delton,
leaner, taller, and older. No time to chin tuck, snatch
a lung of air. True to the book's description,
in her manufactured delirium of drowning,
she climbed my shoulders, then my head.

The wooden rafters wavered above and the black lines
eeled against the turquoise lanes below.
No memory of pressure points, a finger up her nostril,
a thumb in her eyeball. I was empty and drowning.
How quickly the rescuer may need rescuing, but
that wasn't her point. The snot was bored with small
town summer or had wrestled recently with her brother
and lost. Did she sense my kicks were aimed to maim?
that I'd kill her if I could? No, Donna grew bored
with easy prey. I broke surface choking, clung
poolside staring at her, disbelief at what she'd done
but more so at my white-hot hate, my loss
of moral consciousness.

I blew-off senior lifesaving. I didn't find summer boring.
After Donna, I knew I'd never save a drowning soul.

## Untitled (Figure in Landscape)
*Mark Tobey, tempera on illustration board (1935)*

If I recline here
stretch my body across the sharpness of recent rock,
What will erode this night?
I had to come out of my dwelling.
The stone walls, the vaulted ceiling,
crushed me in shadow.
Even my clothes I've abandoned.
I had to know the swells, the obliques
of the larger body beneath me,
had to cover myself with this membrane of light.

A salmon color floods these rocks.
The water below, floured in teal
seems not to flow.
I watch three firs across the chasm
nudge the taupe sky.
Muted in talcum they give up their green,
the anonymity of eggshell light.

I know you see my body, milky, almost shining.
My shoulder, hip, and thigh glow of their own accord.
You cannot see my face, but I tell you, it too, glows.
Even the painter cannot see my face,
does not know my signature.

The moon borrows from the sun
to dust the landscape with pellucid calm
I, too, owe everything.

## Nearly Belonging

*—after Tavares Strachan's "I Belong Here"*

When she leaned over
the water, she found no
face, just a silhouette.
She could cut herself
on a pool this black,
deeper than the vitreous
behind closed eyes.

Black and white
shattered around her in broken
lines instead of line breaks.
Standing waves riffed until
an hourglass of water
with its stopcock set
to ebony let go a drop
and the ringing amplitude
approached an asymptote,
flat lining to gray.

By not looking up,
she could see familiar
stars in the benthos.
There was not never
and not always, only
sometimes, when their
twinkling let her think
she might belong.

## Effluent

Friends walk her to the student health building,
tell the night nurse, *she can't stop*
*crying—she doesn't know why.*
The room she's put in has bars
on the window. They frighten her.
She plays solitaire for hours. She never
wins, the sedative never works.

The unsmiling little
big man sits, legs crossed, pointed
cowboy boot toe aimed
at her. His measured shrink-
speak and glasses too thick
to see through, infuriate her.
Three months of weekly
visits later, he wheedles,
*I look forward to getting to the bottom of this.*
*Do you have a boyfriend?*

Summer, hiding behind a microscope
counting plankton. Barred grids,
5 by 5 fields, 400x power.
At night, nauplii, *biddulphia,*
*Nitszia, coscinodiscus* drift
across her lids, dying in sludge.

She stays awake until Mom and Dad return
from Thursday evening trips hours away.
*Your father's seeing a specialist.*
*It's private, remember that.*

The Zenith radio on low mumbles sundries.
She tries to remember yesterday
or the day before, but the plankton interfere.
Her dad stops mid-routine, toast in hand, and stares
at the eyeholes in her mask. *I've been where you are,*

*looking up at the crescent of sky from*
*the bottom of a shutting manhole.*

She studies harder. She graduates. She lands a job.
On a commute to work she finds herself
behind a soft-spoken middle-aged woman in line
at the Metro kiosk. At the window the woman
pleads to the attendant behind the bars,
*I need to find my body. We've been separated.*
*Please. Tell me what bus to catch.*

## Power Lines

A neon greyhound runs the power lines.
Each crevice in the rock-siding of the station
houses a pigeon, a thin white message
wrapped around one leg.
The pay phone doesn't work.
There are no quarters in the coin return.
The parking meters always show red flags.
You can't see your reflection in the store windows.
You left here yesterday. You left here decades ago.
You know you never left.
A movement at the second story window tells you so.

Those men pinned to benches with ennui
lost themselves the year they never found the body
of the boy who drowned in Goldsborough Creek.
For days they searched the mudflats at low tide.
They still do, confessing to ghost shrimp.
Next to them is the boy who couldn't turn in his friend,
stuck in the furnace vent at Denny's Music Box,
the two of them filching sheet music.
His friend's body discovered by the stench in the storeroom,
salmon rotting on the beach.

*Coca cola* in red italics cannot dilute the salt.
Stones echo heat and the barbershop pole won't spin.
You roam the warm cement at night searching
for coins to pay the meter, or make the call,
the pigeon's message lost.

## Bee Telling

Adjacent to the graves at Mountainview cemetery
stand stacks of white square dressers like headstones
at Arlington. Aligned in reverent unison they face
a prairie of lilies, avalanche and camas.

Humans in hazmats remove
the drawers as if in daydream, as if
radioactivity might actually spill
from such a hum. They examine
the screens, eye to eye with fury.
Do they confess to drones blinking
on the other side? Apologize for stealing
so much oozing, drowsy treacle?

I watch at the field's perimeter
and send a black-edged aerogram, bee
telling. I give them notice that a scourge
wafts in their direction. Exoskeletons
will not be shield enough against
what slumps this way. Fly
to untouched orchards, bury
yourselves in ambrosia, sleep
in lockets of amber.

## On the Runway at SeaTac

She holds her breath, the pause before the pull of gravity
reminds her it's her choice to leave earth willingly to see her son.
She melts into the hug and hears her mum hum *Sweet and Low,*

waking her for breakfast. Hears too the admonitions, *don't walk
the tracks to school, don't take the gully home.* Listens to her dad
before dinner play *Summertime,* the plaintive ostinato in the bass,

his decompression, as the sickly sweet of esters diffuses
from his clothes, and evening coalesces in the yard of the wood
chemist and his family. They sit in the dining room and watch

cedar waxwings while her sister reads Yeats aloud,
the encyclopedia on the sideboard as worn as Bartlett's
Familiar Quotations. The town dwindles. Replacement

trees are sparse and even neap tides flood the tracks. The smell
of Douglas fir and hemlock are usurped by jet fuel, and the music,
by the rush of blood to her ears. The plane lifts off into onshore

flow and there it is, the dog's-leg of an inlet and home just
west of the mill. Her parents never saw the clearcut coming. She sees
the Pacific, their ashes resting on the continental shelf.

### Abandoned Homestead
*Morris Graves, oil on canvas (1937-8)*

As if sheet lightning in the valley beyond
could illuminate the loss, that is how the sunset
also tries to understand who homesteads here.
The greying barn bears remnants of red paint
streaking under eaves and over door,
now a mouth that gapes at desertion.
The pasture patiently fills with tansy.
A black snag frames the clearing,
its lowest branch once sheltering the roof,
now rafters creak under the strain.

Former lives call, hewn from earth
stolen among trees. A husband, leaning
on his mattock, stops to breathe and watch
grey clouds coalesce above the crags.
A wife at the woodstove turns to gaze
toward corn, carrots, beans, and peas
arranged in the patterned garden.
Their children read by lighted kerosene
while firs, longing to carpet this scar,
turn the cabin dark by noon.

The artist sweeps a clearing
from blank canvas, plows furrows
in brushstrokes of oil. Paint encroaches,
hunkers in mauves from the sky,
presses in dark green from the sides,
and takes the space as its own.

**Susan E. Hamilton** was born and raised in Shelton, WA, and now lives in Seattle. Her careers have involved oceanographic cruises, signaling in retinal cone cells, knocking-out a muscarinic receptor, and writing clinical documents. Poetry and painting have accompanied her throughout these careers, exercising the right side of her brain. Her written works have appeared in *Belletrist, Floating Bridge Review, Switched-on Gutenberg, Arnazella, Beyond Parallax, Between the Lines, Signals, West Wind Review,* and other Northwest journals. Her first chapbook, *Informed Consent,* was published by Finishing Line Press in 2018.

www.ingramcontent.com/pod-product-compliance
Lightning Source LLC
Chambersburg PA
CBHW022059080426
42734CB00009B/1415